For Juanita Sampsell

at Christmas 1983

From Preacher and Dottie

as we look ahead to another tour with you!

ISRAEL

A PICTURE BOOK TO REMEMBER HER BY

Designed by
PHILIP CLUCAS MSIAD

Produced by
TED SMART and **DAVID GIBBON**

CRESCENT BOOKS
New York

INTRODUCTION

The scene of some of history's most stirring events, the legendary land of Israel, Yedinat Yesra'el in the ancient Hebrew tongue of its Jewish people, is today a long-awaited dream come true.

As if by a miracle worthy of its Biblical ancestors, out of the empty barren waste and crumbling terraces of not so many years ago, there has again risen a vibrant, pulsating country confident in its role as the world's youngest democracy. With its face turned to the future, Israel is a reflection of the deeply rooted belief and sheer determination of the people who made their return from exile to the land promised to them by God.

Located between two seas, the Mediterranean and the Red Sea, and at the crossroads of Europe and the East, Israel, known previously by many other names, including the Land of Canaan and Palestine, has been subject to continuous upheaval throughout history. Years of being ruled successively by ancient Egyptians, Assyrians, Persians, Greeks, Romans, Arabs, Crusaders, Turks and Britons, led finally to the words of Golda Meir: "There should be some place on earth where we have a Jewish majority..." being fulfilled. On May 14, 1948, a signature was put to the Declaration of Independence which stated, "It is a natural right of the Jewish people, as of all peoples, to command its fate under its own sovereignty."

A visitor to Israel will return home refreshed by a land bursting with spirit, which, although small and with a population of only three million, has welcomed immigrants from all over the world and consequently has a multi-national flavour. Curious in its blend of East and West, remarkably diverse in its people and strikingly beautiful, not necessarily more so than other countries, as one of the early refugees put it, just uniquely so, travellers will undoubtedly leave its shores with some greatly treasured memories.

Not only is the countryside peaceful and inspiring with lush, fertile farmland, dramatic, rugged mountains and burnished desert land, but remnants of its special history in the shape of extensive excavations and unchanged land and seascapes make it a land that feeds the imagination of writers and painters, young people and old alike.

The focal point of three of the world's greatest religions, a constant stream of pilgrims travel to its holy cities; Bethlehem, Nazareth and, of course, Jerusalem, the "jewel" of Israel.

Built on two hills, Jerusalem stands 1,150 metres above the level of the nearby Dead Sea, now a popular location for health resorts. It is the home of the Christian Church of the Holy Sepulchre and the Muslims' third holiest city. For Judaism, a small ruined wall on Temple Hill, a relic of the Temple of Herod now known as the Western Wall, has remained the centre for prayer. Consequently, the city is strictly divisioned according to faith, with each religious group, which include the Armenian, as well as the Jewish, Muslim and Christian, living in their own section.

Elsewhere in the country, there are second and third century synagogues, Crusader towns and fine Byzantine churches with beautifully patterned mosaic floors. But to suggest that Israel, as colourful as its past may be, has only its past to offer, would be wrong. A young state, it has quickly found its feet in the modern competitive world. With a strong emphasis on education there are many fine universities, scientific institutions and cultural centres. As well as the famous Kibbutz, with its unique form of communal living, accommodation includes luxurious hotels, hostels and campsites.

This mixture of "then and now" coupled with a contrasting climate and a multitude of languages make Israel a richly rewarding country.

Above The City of Jerusalem with its crenellated walls, domes, spires and minarets.

Right Jerusalem's Old City by night, with the Jaffa Gate at the far left and the Mount of Olives beyond the City.

Left King David's Hotel and the YMCA building, seen from the Jerusalem Tower Hotel.

Overleaf Jerusalem's Old City with its markets and cave-like shops filled with goods of every description, pictured from the walls by the Damascus Gate; the jumble of television aerials the only sign of modernity.

Below The tombs of the Moslem cemetery. *Right* Adjoining Jerusalem's Jaffa Gate is the Citadel, also known as David's Tower. *Above* The Pyramid of Zachariah and Absalom's Pillar, two of several Second Temple Monuments in the Kidron Valley. *Overleaf* The Golden Gate.

In the narrow streets of Jerusalem's old city are markets and cave-like shops filled with all manner of provisions and goods. *Overleaf* The Church of the Holy Sepulchre in the heart of Jerusalem.

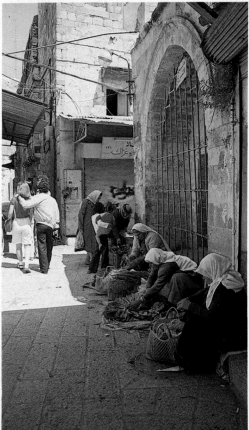

On theses pages is shown the Great Western Wall of the Temple – often referred to as The Wailing Wall – where Jews from all over the world gather to offer prayers.

Overleaf written pleas and prayers are still pushed between the great and ancient stones.

Contrasts in architectural styles are considerable: *above* and *left* the Shrine of the Book which contains The Dead Sea Scrolls discovered *below* in a cave at Qumram. *Bottom right* The Gethsemane Church of All Nations which stands on the lower slopes of the Mount of Olives *overleaf*. The Russian Church of Mary Magdalene is shown *top right*. its onion-shaped domes golden against the blue sky.

One of the most important Islamic holy places is the "Jewel Box of Islam" – the Dome of the Rock – at the heart of Jerusalem's Old City. Some idea of the beauty of the interior of the Dome of the Rock with its mosaic covered walls, may be gathered from the illustration *below*.

Overleaf The bare rock which lies at the heart of the Dome, and from which it takes its name.

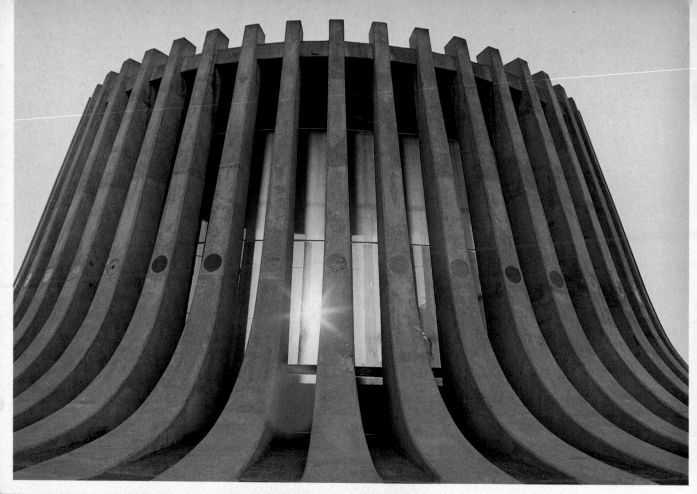

Above, The John F. Kennedy memorial.
Left The eternal flame of the memorial to
the Jews who perished in the European
Holocaust. *Below* The monument to the
Six Day War. *Right* The grave of the
architect of the modern state of Israel,
David Ben-Gurion, and his wife Paula,
overlooking the Negev Desert, seen
overleaf.

Girls recruited into the Israeli armed forces undergo similar training to the men and receive instruction in all manner of modern weaponry including tanks.

These pictures show the extremely important part that agriculture plays in the economy of Israel. Thanks to massive irrigation projects the inhospitable desert has been made to bloom again and bear an abundance of crops, particularly in the many kibbutz and in the area of the Galilee.

Overleaf is shown a field of barley ready for harvesting near Afula.

Above and *below* The recently excavated fortress at Masada which dates back to AD 73. *Right* The ruins of Armageddon and *left* the remains of the Roman Amphitheatre at Beitshean.

The old and the new form the scenery around the shores of the Dead Sea. The barrenness of the area provides a contrast to the irrigated areas of the Negev Desert *overleaf*, with its crops and various cactus.

Israel is a storehouse of archaeological interest including *left* the fortress of Masada; *right* and *below* Caesarea; *above* Castle Nimrod, once occupied by the Crusaders, and *overleaf* Sorek Cave, Absalom's Reserve.

Left The Old City Wall of Tiberias ending at the water's edge. *Above* and *below* From the Coral World Underwater Observatory, excursion boats and glass-bottomed boats set out to view the beautiful and colourful underwater life of this area. *Right* and *bottom right* In the Red Sea just south of Eilat stands Coral Island on which are the remains of Crusader and Mameluke Castles. *Top right* The old fortifications of Acre.

Overleaf Acre's Fisherman's harbour.

The subject of veneration by countless Christian Pilgrims is the Silver Star *left* in the grotto of the Church of the Nativity in Bethlehem *these pages* and *overleaf.* The Mosque on Mount Herodion is pictured *right.*

The miracle of Cana, where Jesus is said to have turned water into wine, is simplistically treated in the Franciscan Church *right* at Kfar Kana. *Left* and *top left* The Church of the Transfiguratiion on Mount Tabor. *Above* and *top* The Cave of the Seventy Elders, showing both the exterior and interior of the cave. *Below* The entrance to the Church of the Nativity, Bethlehem and *overleaf* Nazareth in the Galilee.

Tel Aviv has all the ingredients for an ideal resort as seen *right;* excellent beaches and *left* a marina for pleasure craft. *Below* and *overleaf* Tel Aviv the largest, most modern and fastest growing city in Israel, and *above* the city of technology, Haifa.